WISCONSIN BADGERS

BY MARTY GITLIN

Published by ABDO Publishing Company, PO Box 398166, Minneapolis, MN 55439. Copyright © 2013 by Abdo Consulting Group, Inc. International copyrights reserved in all countries. No part of this book may be reproduced in any form without written permission from the publisher. SportsZone™ is a trademark and logo of ABDO Publishing Company.

Printed in the United States of America,
North Mankato, Minnesota
102012
012013

Editor: Chrös McDougall
Series Designer: Craig Hinton

Photo Credits: Morry Gash/AP Images, Cover, 37; Reed Saxon/AP Images, 1; Kevork Djansezian/ AP Images, 4, 42 (bottom right); Vincent Laforet/Allsport/Getty Images, 7, 9; Donald Miralle/Allsport, 11; David Stluka/AP Images, 12, 19, 39, 42 (top), 43 (top right and bottom), 44; Bain News Service/ Library of Congress, 15; University of Wisconsin/AP Images, 20; AP Images, 23, 25, 26, 31, 43 (top left); Lois Bernstein/AP Images, 29, 42 (bottom left); Andy Manis/AP Images, 33, 34; Ben Liebenberg/AP Images, 41

Cataloging-in-Publication Data
Gitlin, Marty.
 Wisconsin Badgers / Marty Gitlin.
   p. cm. -- (Inside college football)
Includes bibliographical references and index.
ISBN 978-1-61783-658-9
1. Wisconsin Badgers (Football team)--History--Juvenile literature. 2. University of Wisconsin-- Madison--Football--History--Juvenile literature. I. Title.
796.332--dc15

                                                    2012945713

TABLE OF CONTENTS

1 BEATING THE BRUINS 5

2 THE BADGERS' BEGINNINGS 13

3 GOOD TEAMS, BAD TEAMS 21

4 BARRY BOOSTS THE BADGERS 27

5 BRET TAKES OVER 35

TIMELINE 42

QUICK STATS 44

QUOTES & ANECDOTES 45

GLOSSARY 46

FOR MORE INFORMATION 47

INDEX 48

ABOUT THE AUTHOR 48

Wisconsin running back Ron Dayne celebrates after scoring his third touchdown in the 1999 Rose Bowl.

BEATING THE BRUINS

IT WAS JANUARY 1, 1999. MILLIONS OF AMERICANS WERE CELEBRATING NEW YEAR'S DAY. THE WISCONSIN BADGERS FOOTBALL TEAM WANTED TO CELEBRATE AS WELL. BUT IT COULD NOT—NOT YET ANYWAY. FIRST IT HAD TO BEAT THE UNIVERSITY OF CALIFORNIA, LOS ANGELES (UCLA) BRUINS IN THE ROSE BOWL. THEN THE TEAM COULD CELEBRATE NEW YEAR'S DAY AND A GREAT VICTORY.

Before the game, TV analyst Craig James called the Badgers "the worst team to ever play in the Rose Bowl." This angered the Wisconsin players. The Rose Bowl is the oldest bowl game. It has a rich history filled with great teams and traditions. The Wisconsin players wanted to prove James wrong.

They were doing just that with one minute left in the game. The Badgers were leading the Bruins 38–31. UCLA had the ball on the Wisconsin 47-yard line. But it was fourth down. The Badgers only needed one stop to seal the victory.

TOM TERRIFIC

Wisconsin senior defensive lineman Tom Burke enjoyed one of the best seasons in school history in 1998. He recorded 22 sacks. He also made 31 tackles that resulted in negative yards for an opponent. It came as no surprise when he was named the Big Ten Conference Defensive Player of the Year. Burke went on to play four seasons for the Arizona Cardinals in the National Football League (NFL).

Bruins quarterback Cade McNown took the snap from center. Wisconsin defensive ends Tom Burke and John Favret broke free from their blockers. They began chasing McNown, who was forced to run. Then freshman defensive tackle Wendell Bryant slammed him to the ground.

It was over. The Badgers had beaten the Bruins and proven James wrong. They finished the season ranked sixth in the nation with an 11–1 record. And they had Bryant to thank for it.

"I didn't know we had the game won until I got to the sideline and all the guys were jumping up and down," Bryant said. "Then I looked up at the clock and I realized it was over. What a way to wind up my freshman season at Wisconsin."

The game also was a fitting end to junior Ron Dayne's season. The powerful 250-pound running back steamrolled into the end zone for four touchdowns. He rushed for an incredible 246 yards as well—one yard short of the all-time Rose Bowl record. It was no wonder he was voted the game's Most Valuable Player.

Dayne was used to such success. He had been running over defenders since arriving at Wisconsin two years earlier. But his performance against UCLA was especially sweet. After all, some complained that Dayne had slipped that season. He had exploded onto the scene as a freshman by rushing for 1,863 yards and 18 touchdowns. He averaged an incredible 6.3 yards per carry that season.

His numbers dropped as a sophomore and again as a junior. But the Bruins learned the hard way that Dayne still was a great running back.

[7]

DAYNE AND THE DISCUS

Burly Wisconsin running back Ron Dayne was not just a great football player. He also was one of the best high school discus throwers in history. Dayne tossed the discus more than 216 feet (65.84 m) in 1996 for Overlook Regional High School in New Jersey. It was the third-longest throw ever recorded by a US high school athlete. He also won the shot put event at the famous Penn Relays. That qualified Dayne for the US Olympic Trials. But he turned down a shot at the Olympic Games to play college football.

And they were surprised that he did not rely only on his strength to beat them.

"He can overpower you," said UCLA linebacker Tony White. "But then when you think he's going to overpower you, he uses his finesse and makes you miss. I don't think we've seen a running back like that all year."

Dayne and Bryant were among many stars for Wisconsin in the victory. Freshman defensive back Jamar Fletcher made one of the game's biggest plays. He gave Wisconsin a 38–28 lead early in the fourth quarter when he ran back an interception 47 yards for a touchdown.

The Rose Bowl proved to be a fitting end for a dream 1998 season. But the trip to Pasadena, California, almost did not happen. The Badgers won their first nine games of the 1998 season. Their defense was among the best in the nation, giving up just seven points or less in six of those victories. But a 27–10 loss to Michigan in the tenth week of the season ruined the Badgers' chance to play for the national championship.

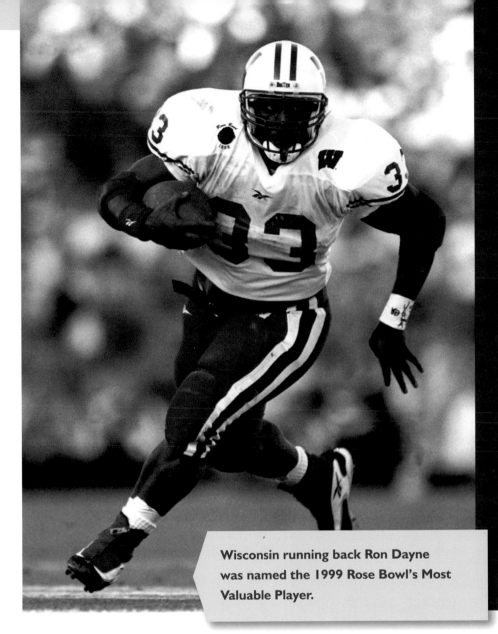

Wisconsin running back Ron Dayne was named the 1999 Rose Bowl's Most Valuable Player.

It also forced Wisconsin to beat Penn State the next week to earn a Rose Bowl berth. It was not an easy victory. The Nittany Lions were ranked sixteenth in the country.

But the Badgers responded with their best performance of the season. Burke chased Penn State quarterback Kevin Thompson all over

THREE-SPORT STAR

Chris Chambers excelled in football, basketball, and track in high school. He even won the state title in the 400-meter dash. Wisconsin offered Chambers a scholarship to play wide receiver for the football team. But he also yearned to play basketball. He made Wisconsin's basketball team as a freshman.

Chambers stuck to football after that first year. He averaged an incredible 20.1 yards per catch in 1998. He continued to shine with the Badgers. Then he surprised many football experts by emerging as an NFL star. The Miami Dolphins selected Chambers after 51 other players were taken in the 2000 NFL Draft. But he performed better than many of them. He averaged 63 catches for 879 yards during his first six years in the NFL. He caught 82 passes for 1,118 yards and 11 touchdowns in 2005. His performance that year earned him a spot in the Pro Bowl.

the field and recorded four sacks. Dayne received plenty of help running the ball from Mike Samuel, who rushed for 89 yards and a fourth-quarter touchdown. The senior running back also threw a 26-yard scoring strike to sophomore wide receiver Chris Chambers. With the victory, the Badgers were indeed heading to the Rose Bowl.

Now it was up to coach Barry Alvarez and the players to prepare for UCLA. Alvarez knew his team was still disappointed about the loss to Michigan earlier in the season. So he tried to inspire his players and give them confidence. He pointed out that the Bruins were in the same boat. They, too, had lost a game earlier in the year that had ended their national title hopes.

Few gave the Badgers a chance to win. Most considered the Bruins a better team, and the game was being played in the Rose Bowl—UCLA's home stadium. But Wisconsin backers were not to be outdone. They traveled in

droves from Madison and other Wisconsin cities to California. More than half of the fans at the stadium on that New Year's Day were cheering for Wisconsin. It was a game Samuel will never forget.

"The Rose Bowl was magical," he said. "It was [strange] out there, just enjoying and reflecting on it. You just relish the moment, knowing that opportunities like this don't come around every day. So you want to make the most of it, and that's what we did as a team. . . . To us, it was the event of a lifetime, and we seized the opportunity."

Wisconsin teams had not always seized their opportunities over the years. But the Badgers did start out with a bang.

BEATING THE BRUINS

These days, Camp Randall Stadium is known for having one of the most lively atmospheres in the nation.

2

THE BADGERS' BEGINNINGS

THE WISCONSIN BADGERS PLAY THEIR HOME FOOTBALL GAMES AT CAMP RANDALL STADIUM. THE STADIUM WAS NAMED AFTER FORMER WISCONSIN GOVERNOR ALEXANDER W. RANDALL. BUT HE DIED 22 YEARS BEFORE THE BADGERS FIRST PLAYED A GAME OF FOOTBALL IN THAT STADIUM IN 1894. IN FACT, WISCONSIN DID NOT PLAY ITS FIRST FOOTBALL GAME UNTIL 1889.

Camp Randall was built in 1861 as a training center for Union troops during the Civil War. Approximately 1,400 Confederate troops were held there as prisoners the next year.

The war was a distant memory in 1894, though. That is when Wisconsin beat Minnesota 6–0 in the first football game played at Camp Randall. The victory ended a 5–2 season for the Badgers. And they just kept on winning. Phil King took over as Wisconsin's coach in 1896. The team won 16 of 19 games during those two seasons under King, recording

14 shutouts along the way. They won the first two Western Conference titles in 1896 and 1897 with a stout defense.

One star of those early teams was Australian kicker Pat O'Dea. He booted 14 field goals in 1897 and earned the nickname "The Kangaroo Kicker." But perhaps the best Badger bunch of that era played in 1901. They won all nine games that season and outscored their opponents 317–5. It is no wonder that they again captured the Western Conference crown.

Football in its early days was more chaotic than today's game. The games were sometimes very brutal. The number of games each team played often varied as well. But Wisconsin was generally successful during its early years. The team went unbeaten in 1906. And it posted winning records every year from 1891 until 1910.

Many talented players suited up for Wisconsin in its early years. Nine of its players earned All-Western Conference honors in 1912 under new coach Bill Juneau. But arguably no player was better than two-way lineman Bob Butler. He was a great blocker and tackler. Butler later earned a spot in the College Football Hall of Fame.

Butler led the 1912 team to another undefeated season. It was the school's last undefeated season through 2011. The Badgers maintained their early tradition of strong defense that year. They gave up just 29 points in seven games and shut out four opponents.

Fans flocked in droves to see their beloved Badgers play. The home field only seated 3,000, but as many as 12,000 others would stand on the

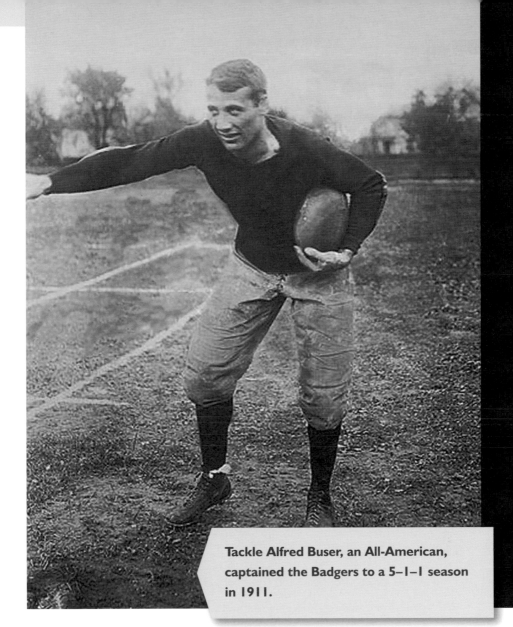

Tackle Alfred Buser, an All-American, captained the Badgers to a 5–1–1 season in 1911.

sidelines. Construction of a new Camp Randall began in 1915. But the new stadium would open too late.

The school used temporary bleachers to seat thousands of fans for a showdown against rival Minnesota on November 20, 1915. However, reports said that the stands caved while holding thousands of people in the second quarter. The dedication of the new Camp Randall Stadium two years later, in 1917, was a much happier event. More than 10,000 fans safely watched Wisconsin's 10–7 win over Minnesota.

The Badgers usually fielded strong teams through 1932. They suffered just two losing seasons during that period, and they contended for Western Conference titles regularly. But they just could not win the big game.

The Badgers continued to shut down opponents with a premier defense. They peaked in 1928 by giving up just 38 points in nine games. Only a 6–0 loss to Minnesota in the final game of the season prevented Wisconsin from winning the league championship.

Clarence Spears replaced Glenn Thistlethwaite as coach in 1932, and the team initially continued winning. The Badgers managed an impressive 6–1–1 record that year. So few could have imagined the collapse that would soon follow. Wisconsin compiled just a 26–40–3 record over the next nine seasons.

The Badgers needed great players to turn around the team. And they landed one of the best in college football in 1942. Halfback Elroy Hirsch was nicknamed "Crazy Legs" for his running style. Defenders could not figure out which direction he was about to move. Hirsch rushed for 767 yards and five touchdowns that season.

Hirsch was not alone in helping turn around the offense. All-American end Dave Schreiner and fullback Pat Harder played major roles as well. But it was the defense that really transformed Wisconsin into a national power. It gave up 26 points per game in 1941 but just 6.8 in 1942.

The Badgers played arguably their biggest game to that point on October 31, 1942. They were unranked to start the season, but they had risen to sixth in the country since then. Opponent Ohio State was ranked number one. The game received national attention. It was broadcast

"CRAZY LEGS"

Elroy "Crazy Legs" Hirsch played just one year with Wisconsin. He soon left to play for Michigan before going to the Chicago Rockets of the All-America Football Conference in 1946. When Hirsch began his professional career, he had a hard time making the most of his "crazy legs." As a running back, he was often tackled before he reached open space.

Hirsch did little with the Rockets during his first three years as a professional. But when he joined the Los Angeles Rams, he was moved to wide receiver. There he blossomed into one of the best players ever to play that position. He peaked in 1951 by leading the league in catches (66), receiving yards (1,495), and touchdowns (17). Hirsch was voted into the Pro Football Hall of Fame. But he remained modest.

"I'm just a busted-down, retreaded halfback who happened to get lucky," he said.

THE BADGERS' BEGINNINGS

on the radio to 187 stations, including 11 in South America and two in England. Approximately 9,000 Wisconsin fans celebrated Halloween with a "We Can't Lose" pep rally the night before.

Most believed Wisconsin could, and would, lose. Coach Harry Stuhldreher was considered no match for Ohio State counterpart Paul Brown. After all, Brown would emerge as one of the most legendary figures in the history of football.

But the Badgers had other ideas. They grabbed a 10–0 halftime lead and cruised to a 17–7 victory. Hirsch and Harder buried the Buckeyes with a combined 215 rushing yards.

The Badgers moved up to second in the nation after that game. But they could not manage to hold on to that high ranking. An average Iowa team upset the Badgers the following week. And Ohio State went on to win the national championship despite losing to Wisconsin.

Fewer Americans than usual were paying attention to college football at that time. And fewer young men were available to play

STORY BEHIND THE NICKNAME

During the 1830s, Wisconsin miners lived in caves carved into the hills. These caves were described as "badger dens" and the miners as "badgers." The nickname was later applied to all Wisconsin residents. Wisconsin eventually became known as "The Badger State." So the University of Wisconsin adopted the Badgers as its nickname as well.

Bucky the Badger has been representing Wisconsin sports since 1949. Different mascots roamed the sidelines before then.

the sport. Thousands were fighting for the United States overseas in World War II.

The Badgers continued to win after the war ended in 1945. But still, they just could not win enough to achieve greatness.

Guard Jerry Smith played for Wisconsin in the early 1950s, before a long career coaching in the NFL.

3

GOOD TEAMS, BAD TEAMS

THE BADGERS WERE USUALLY A BETTER-THAN-AVERAGE TEAM AFTER WORLD WAR II ENDED IN 1945. THEIR DEFENSE REMAINED ONE OF THE BEST IN THE COUNTRY. YET THEY STILL COULD NOT WIN ENOUGH GAMES TO CONTEND FOR A NATIONAL CHAMPIONSHIP. ONE LOSS OFTEN COST THEM DEARLY. SOMETIMES THE DEFEAT WOULD OCCUR EARLY IN THE SEASON. SOMETIMES IT CAME LATE. BUT IT ALWAYS HAPPENED AT SOME POINT.

One example was 1951. Wisconsin's defense led the nation in allowing just 154.8 yards per game. And it surrendered just 5.9 points per game. But a 14–10 loss to Illinois cost the Badgers the Western Conference title. They finished the year with a 7–1–1 record.

Wisconsin beat Illinois early in 1952. That skyrocketed the Badgers to the top of the national rankings for the first time. But then they lost to Ohio State the following week. Wisconsin tied Purdue for the Western Conference crown that season. However, the Badgers fell to the University of Southern California (USC) in the Rose Bowl. It was Wisconsin's first berth in the famous game that traditionally features the Big Ten and Pacific-12 champions. The Big Ten was called the Western Conference until 1953.

Meanwhile, the performance of arguably the greatest Badger of all was being wasted. Fullback Alan Ameche took college football by storm during the early 1950s. He made an immediate impact in 1951 during his first year on the team. Ameche became the first freshman to lead the Big Ten in rushing yards. He broke the conference record with 774 yards on the ground that season.

Ameche was just warming up, too. He shattered his own mark a year later by rushing for 1,079 yards. That included 133 rushing yards in the Rose Bowl. His production as a running back dropped the next two years when he also was forced to play defense. But he was praised for his work as a linebacker.

In 1954, Ameche earned the coveted Heisman Trophy. It is presented each year to the best player in college football. He later was voted into the College Football Hall of Fame.

VICTIM OF WAR

Star end Dave Schreiner never returned to play for Wisconsin. He was one of more than 200,000 Americans who lost their lives in World War II. A sniper killed Schreiner while he was serving in the Marines in 1945—the last year of the war. He wrote many letters home to his parents and sister that were later published.

Despite Ameche's success, Wisconsin only went to one bowl game during his time there—the Rose Bowl after the 1952 season. The Badgers slipped a bit after Ameche left, falling as low as 1–5–3 in 1956. But they sported winning records six times and qualified for the Rose Bowl twice from 1957 to 1963.

The Badgers also featured tight end Pat Richter. He was one of the finest players in the country. Richter twice led the Big Ten in receiving—topping the nation as a junior in 1962. A victory over top-ranked Northwestern that year clinched a berth in the Rose Bowl.

Wisconsin suffered through a couple of bad seasons in the mid-1960s. But this time, they did not bounce back under coach Milt Bruhn.

GOOD TEAMS, BAD TEAMS

SPECIAL PLAYER, SPECIAL MAN

Alan Ameche enjoyed the journey through life after starring with the Badgers. He proved to be a great NFL player and a generous man.

Ameche was the third player selected in the 1955 NFL Draft. The Baltimore Colts paid him $15,000 to sign, the most ever offered to a rookie to that point. He justified their faith in him. Ameche sprinted 79 yards for a touchdown the first time he touched the ball. He led the league with 961 rushing yards and nine touchdowns in his first season. A leg injury cut his career short. But he made an estimated $19 million after helping launch a hamburger restaurant chain. He donated much of that money to a variety of charities.

"No one ever had a bad word to say about [Ameche]," said former Colts teammate Art Donovan. "The things he would do for people, out of the goodness of his heart, were amazing."

John Coatta replaced Bruhn in 1967. However, the Badgers only got worse. In fact, Wisconsin did not win a single game during the next two years.

The Badgers finally showed some improvement with a 3–7 season in 1969. But a long period of mediocrity continued after John Jardine took over as coach in 1970. It also continued under coach Dave McClain, who replaced Jardine in 1978 and remained until 1985.

During that time, Wisconsin did not finish a season more than three games over or under .500. However, McClain did coach the team to three straight winning seasons during the early 1980s.

Amidst the mediocrity, there was one breakthrough. After four bowl game defeats, the Badgers finally won one in 1982. Wisconsin was barely eligible for a bowl game at 6–5. One of those wins was a 6–0 victory at Ohio State. The Badgers had not beaten the Buckeyes on the road since 1918.

The Badgers were ready when the Independence Bowl rolled around. Quarterback Randy Wright overcame rare below-zero temperatures in Shreveport, Louisiana. He threw two touchdown passes to lead Wisconsin to a 14–3 victory over Kansas State.

McClain had the program heading in the right direction. And he was very popular among the players. However, he died unexpectedly at age 48 in 1986.

Wisconsin compiled a woeful 9–36 record over the next four years. The team searched for a coach in 1990 who could transform the Badgers into a winning team. It found one. Wisconsin was about to join the elite in college football.

GOOD TEAMS, BAD TEAMS

After years of mediocrity, Wisconsin's fortunes finally changed after Barry Alvarez took over as coach in 1990.

4

BARRY BOOSTS THE BADGERS

THE WISCONSIN FOOTBALL PROGRAM HIT A LOW POINT TWO DAYS AFTER THANKSGIVING IN 1989. ONLY 29,000 FANS SHOWED UP TO WATCH AS THE BADGERS FINISHED THEIR SEASON BY LOSING BADLY TO MICHIGAN STATE.

They ended the year with a 2–9 record. It was hard to believe that was one *more* victory than they had recorded the year before. The Badgers were one of the worst teams in the country. Something had to be done.

After the 1989 season, Barry Alvarez was named the new coach. Alvarez had been a highly successful assistant at Notre Dame. He had helped the Fighting Irish win 23 games in a row from 1988 to 1989.

Alvarez understood that the Wisconsin program was a mess. When introduced as coach to the media, he admitted that the team would take time to fix. But he added that fans would soon be excited about the team.

PLAYING FOR AN AXE

The Wisconsin Badgers and the Minnesota Golden Gophers boast the longest rivalry in college football. They played 121 times between 1890 and 2011. The winner every year is presented with the Paul Bunyan's Axe Trophy. It is a huge axe inscribed with the words "Paul Bunyan Football Trophy." Bunyan was a legendary fictional lumberjack who carried around an axe. The axe was not always given to the annual winner, though. From 1930 to 1943, the Minnesota-Wisconsin game was played for the "Slab of Bacon." That was a piece of wood displaying a picture of a football.

"They better get season tickets now, because before long they won't be able to," he said.

Alvarez was right on both counts. The Badgers did not improve overnight. They lost 10 of 11 games in his first year. Their record since coach Dave McClain died was 10–46. But then Alvarez began recruiting some of the best high school players in the nation. He was serious about winning. He meant business—and he made sure his players did as well.

Pretty soon, the Badgers indeed began improving. They could hardly have gotten any worse. But the speed in which they grew into a national power was stunning. The Badgers won five games in 1991 and 1992 before winning 10 games and tying for the Big Ten title the following year.

Suddenly, stars were shining all over the field in 1993. Sophomore quarterback Darrell Bevell took over as a starter that year. His career ended with school records in passing yards and touchdowns.

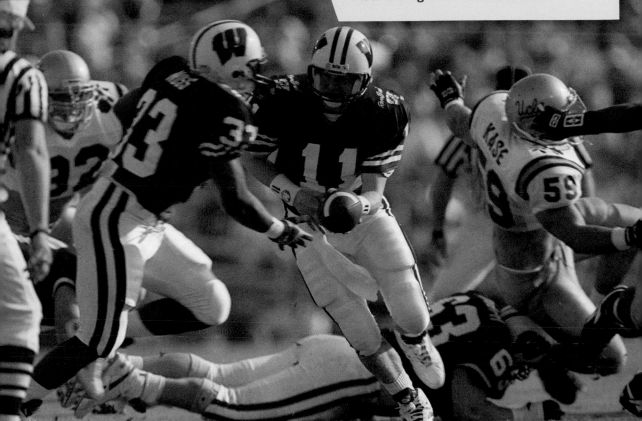

Running back Brent Moss rushed for 1,637 yards and 16 touchdowns. Linebackers Pete Monty and Tarek Saleh were showing the talents that earned them NFL careers. And so was All-American center Cory Raymer.

Three years after sporting a 1–10 record, the Badgers were playing UCLA in the Rose Bowl on January 1, 1994. Every player knew what a victory would mean for Wisconsin football. After all, the program had been laughed at for years.

BARRY BOOSTS THE BADGERS

"We all understood the history and how much a part of history we were," Bevell said. "[We understood that] we could turn the tide for Wisconsin and win it."

The Badgers knew that they would need a big game from Moss. The Bruins quickly realized why he had been named Big Ten Player of the Year. The bruising running back ran all over them. He rushed for 158 yards and two touchdowns that gave his team a 14–3 lead. When the final second ticked off the game clock, the scoreboard said it all: Wisconsin 21, UCLA 16.

The Badgers finished that season ranked sixth in the country. They soon became used to earning lofty rankings. Alvarez continued to recruit talented players. Those players performed well for the next few years. Then Wisconsin followed up its great 1998 season with another Rose Bowl victory over UCLA.

The 1999 Badgers thrived despite a brutal schedule. They beat four ranked teams in Ohio State, Minnesota, Michigan State, and Purdue.

BADGER HEROES

Wisconsin fullback Kevin Ellison and defensive back Dennis Tillman became heroes in September 1990. The sophomores were visiting a friend when they noticed that the home had been broken into. Drawers had been opened and clothing tossed about. They noticed a man hiding under the bed. They grabbed him and held him until police arrived. They later learned that police also wanted the man for stabbing a young girl. The two Badgers became famous. They were featured on the TV show *America's Most Wanted*.

Wisconsin quarterback Brooks Bollinger looks for a receiver during the 2000 Rose Bowl against Stanford.

And they dominated opponent after opponent. Wisconsin battered Ohio State 42–17. It thrashed Indiana 59–0. It clobbered Michigan State 40–10. And it whipped Iowa 41–3.

The Badgers also won their first undisputed Big Ten title, which again sent them to the Rose Bowl. No Big Ten team had ever won two straight

"ON, WISCONSIN"

The Wisconsin Badgers have long featured one of the most famous fight songs. Chicago native William Purdy composed "On, Wisconsin" in 1909. He planned to submit the song with a different title to the University of Minnesota. That school was offering $100 for a new fight song. A fraternity brother named Carl Beck had another idea, though. He offered to write words to Purdy's song and send it to Wisconsin, where Beck had attended school.

The tune was embraced immediately at Wisconsin. Military bands and approximately 2,500 other schools later played it. It was sung for the first time during the 1909 homecoming game against Minnesota.

Rose Bowls. But the Badgers were now considered a national power, and they had a chance. They were ranked fourth in the country. Though Rose Bowl foe Stanford was tough, few believed Wisconsin would lose.

The Badgers quickly faced a challenge, though. They played poorly in the first half and trailed 9–3. But senior running back Ron Dayne and the defense rose to the occasion. Dayne steamrolled over the Stanford defenders and finished the game with 200 rushing yards. The Wisconsin defense held Stanford to minus-5 rushing yards and zero points in the second half. The result was a 17–9 victory. *Now* there was a Big Ten team with two straight Rose Bowl wins.

"There's nothing like doing something that no one else has done," Alvarez said. "You don't get many opportunities like that in a lifetime."

The Badgers continued to win and earn trips to bowl games after that. Stars such as wide receiver Lee Evans, cornerback Jamar Fletcher, and defensive end Erasmus James led a new generation of winners.

Alvarez would not coach the Badgers to another Big Ten title or Rose Bowl. But he stepped down as coach on a high note. He coached the team to a 10–3 record in 2005 and a Capital One Bowl victory. He quit coaching after that. But he did not quit on Wisconsin sports. Instead, he remained at the school as full-time athletic director.

Assistant coach Bret Bielema was promoted to head coach. Some feared the loss of Alvarez on the sideline would mean more losses on the field. But that fear quickly disappeared. The Badgers did not miss a beat.

Wisconsin offensive tackle Joe Thomas protects running back P. J. Hill from defenders during a 2006 game.

5

BRET TAKES OVER

ALL EYES WERE ON BRET BIELEMA. BARRY ALVAREZ HAD ENTRUSTED BIELEMA TO BE THE NEW WISCONSIN FOOTBALL COACH. ALVAREZ HAD TURNED THE BADGERS INTO ONE OF THE FINEST TEAMS IN THE COUNTRY. BIELEMA COULD NOT ALLOW THEM TO SLIP.

Alvarez had left Bielema with tremendous talent in 2006. Wisconsin carried on its tradition of producing great offensive linemen. Senior tackle Joe Thomas won the Outland Trophy that year. It is presented to the top offensive lineman in college football each year.

Thomas later blossomed into one of the best players in the NFL. He was one of many 2006 Badgers to forge NFL careers. Other Wisconsin players who later reached the NFL included linebackers Jonathan Casillas and DeAndre Levy, defensive linemen Nick Hayden and Matt Shaughnessy, and tight end Travis Beckum.

NO ORDINARY JOE

Offensive linemen usually receive less attention than quarterbacks, running backs, and other skill players. But linemen play an important role on any football team. Offensive tackle Joe Thomas might have been the best of many great offensive linemen to play at Wisconsin. The Cleveland Browns selected him third in the 2007 NFL Draft. That made Thomas the highest NFL Draft pick in Wisconsin history. And he emerged immediately as one of the best linemen in the NFL. Thomas earned a spot in the Pro Bowl in each of his first five seasons with the Browns.

It was no wonder the Badgers enjoyed one of their best seasons. They won nine straight games after a loss to Michigan in the fourth week. They were ranked sixth in the country when they met twelfth-ranked Arkansas in the Capital One Bowl.

Critics claimed Wisconsin played an easy schedule. After all, the Badgers had not beaten a ranked team all season. The Badgers had something to prove. And they proved it.

Arkansas shut down the Wisconsin running attack. But Badgers senior quarterback John Stocco was not to be stopped in his last college game. He threw two touchdown passes in the first half of a 17–14 victory. One of the scoring strikes was to Beckum, who caught five passes for 82 yards.

Bielema knew Alvarez would be proud. "My guess is that there will be several messages on my cell phone from coach Alvarez," Bielema joked after the victory.

Wisconsin quarterback John Stocco hands the ball off to running back P. J. Hill during a 2006 game.

Wisconsin fans no longer had to worry about Bielema's coaching abilities. But he still had to prove he could recruit good players. And he did just that in the years that followed the bowl win over Arkansas.

One player Bielema recruited who made a huge impact was tackle Gabe Carimi. Carimi replaced Thomas, who left for the NFL in 2007. Carimi matched Thomas and upheld the tradition of great Wisconsin offensive linemen by winning the 2010 Outland Trophy.

A TRADITIONAL DANCE

Wisconsin fans, band members, and even players do an unusual dance between the third and fourth quarters of home games. They jump in unison to a 1990s hip-hop song called "Jump Around." Even players on opposing teams have joined in. The singing and dancing get so loud that Camp Randall Stadium actually shakes.

Carimi anchored arguably the best offensive line in college football. He and fellow linemen John Moffitt and Bill Nagy all wound up in the NFL. Their blocking helped the 2010 Badgers blossom into one of the most explosive offensive teams in the country. The defense was not as strong, but defensive end J. J. Watt was among the best in the nation.

The blockers opened up huge holes for the ground attack. Running backs John Clay, James White, and Montee Ball combined for 3,060 yards rushing and 46 touchdowns in the 2010 season.

The Badgers averaged an incredible 41.5 points per game. They scored 70 points in wins over Austin Peay and Northwestern, and 83 points in clobbering Indiana. But their best performance was against top-ranked Ohio State on the night of October 16. Senior wide receiver David Gilreath sprinted 97 yards for a touchdown on the opening kickoff. Clay then followed with two touchdown runs. White eluded two Buckeye tacklers for a 12-yard touchdown that gave the Badgers a 28–18 lead. That clinched one of the biggest wins in the history of Wisconsin football.

"I know this isn't a bowl game or the national championship game," said junior safety Aaron Henry. "But I just started crying. . . . Nobody really expected us to go out there and win. It's an unbelievable feeling. I wish this night could last forever."

The pleasant feeling remained with the Badgers until January 1, 2011. They swept through the rest of the regular season unbeaten and climbed to number four in the national rankings. Awaiting them in the Rose Bowl was undefeated Texas Christian University (TCU).

The showdown remained close from beginning to end. The Badgers trailed 21–19 after Ball scored a touchdown with two minutes left.

LIKE FATHER, LIKE SON

Wide receiver Al Toon did not receive a great opportunity to show his talent during the early 1980s. The Badgers of that era did not often throw the ball. But Toon did set school career records in catches (131), receiving yards (2,103), and receiving touchdowns (19). And he was just warming up. Toon blossomed into one of the best wide receivers in the NFL during eight seasons with the New York Jets.

Badger fans were not done cheering for Toons. Al's son, Nick Toon, arrived at Wisconsin in 2008. He took advantage of an offense that emphasized the pass. He caught 171 passes for 2,447 yards in four years with the Badgers. NFL scouts took notice when he caught 10 touchdown passes as a senior. The New Orleans Saints selected him in the fourth round of the 2012 NFL Draft.

Wisconsin attempted a two-point conversion that could tie the game. Senior quarterback Scott Tolzien spotted tight end Jacob Pedersen open just past the goal line. TCU linebacker Tank Carder was blocked as he rushed in, but he managed to leap in the air and bat down the pass.

It was over. The Badgers had lost a heartbreaker. Bielema just hoped his players could bounce back from it.

"Hopefully the scar that we're going to take from this game can get us back [to the Rose Bowl] sooner than later," he said.

Bielema had nothing to worry about. His Badgers indeed returned to the Rose Bowl the next season. Quarterback Russell Wilson had transferred to Wisconsin from North Carolina State. He emerged as perhaps the best quarterback in school history. He threw for 3,175 yards and 33 touchdowns with just four interceptions that season.

Wilson also spent plenty of time handing the ball to Ball. The junior led the nation with 1,923 rushing yards. He also tied a Division I record with 39 touchdowns.

The Badgers rolled over their first six opponents. One of those was a highly anticipated game against eighth-ranked Nebraska. It was the Cornhuskers' first game in the Big Ten. Wisconsin rose to number four in the national rankings. But Michigan State and Ohio State then upset the Badgers. They also lost to Oregon in the Rose Bowl.

The defeats disappointed Badgers fans. But they could remember just 25 years earlier when they could only dream of playing in bowl games.

BRET TAKES OVER

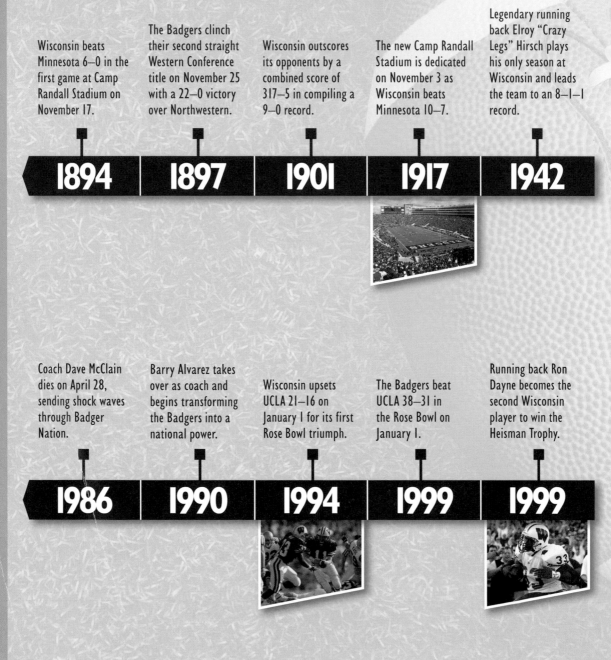

Wisconsin beats Minnesota 6–0 in the first game at Camp Randall Stadium on November 17.

1894

The Badgers clinch their second straight Western Conference title on November 25 with a 22–0 victory over Northwestern.

1897

Wisconsin outscores its opponents by a combined score of 317–5 in compiling a 9–0 record.

1901

The new Camp Randall Stadium is dedicated on November 3 as Wisconsin beats Minnesota 10–7.

1917

Legendary running back Elroy "Crazy Legs" Hirsch plays his only season at Wisconsin and leads the team to an 8–1–1 record.

1942

Coach Dave McClain dies on April 28, sending shock waves through Badger Nation.

1986

Barry Alvarez takes over as coach and begins transforming the Badgers into a national power.

1990

Wisconsin upsets UCLA 21–16 on January 1 for its first Rose Bowl triumph.

1994

The Badgers beat UCLA 38–31 in the Rose Bowl on January 1.

1999

Running back Ron Dayne becomes the second Wisconsin player to win the Heisman Trophy.

1999

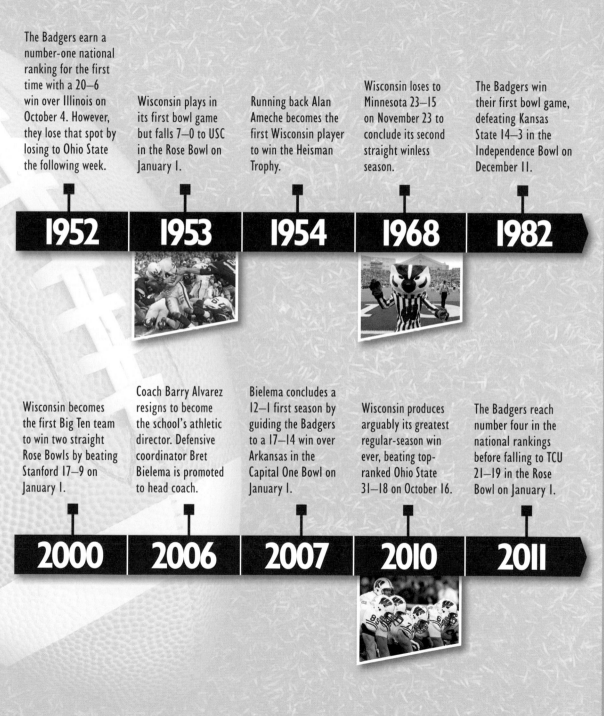

The Badgers earn a number-one national ranking for the first time with a 20–6 win over Illinois on October 4. However, they lose that spot by losing to Ohio State the following week.

Wisconsin plays in its first bowl game but falls 7–0 to USC in the Rose Bowl on January 1.

Running back Alan Ameche becomes the first Wisconsin player to win the Heisman Trophy.

Wisconsin loses to Minnesota 23–15 on November 23 to conclude its second straight winless season.

The Badgers win their first bowl game, defeating Kansas State 14–3 in the Independence Bowl on December 11.

1952 1953 1954 1968 1982

Wisconsin becomes the first Big Ten team to win two straight Rose Bowls by beating Stanford 17–9 on January 1.

Coach Barry Alvarez resigns to become the school's athletic director. Defensive coordinator Bret Bielema is promoted to head coach.

Bielema concludes a 12–1 first season by guiding the Badgers to a 17–14 win over Arkansas in the Capital One Bowl on January 1.

Wisconsin produces arguably its greatest regular-season win ever, beating top-ranked Ohio State 31–18 on October 16.

The Badgers reach number four in the national rankings before falling to TCU 21–19 in the Rose Bowl on January 1.

2000 2006 2007 2010 2011

QUICK STATS

PROGRAM INFO
University of Wisconsin Badgers (1889–)

NATIONAL CHAMPIONSHIPS
None

OTHER ACHIEVEMENTS
BCS bowl appearances (1999–): 3
Western Conference/Big Ten
    championships (1896–): 13
Bowl record: 11–12

HEISMAN TROPHY WINNERS
Alan Ameche, 1954
Ron Dayne, 1999

KEY PLAYERS
(POSITION[S]; SEASONS WITH TEAM)
Alan Ameche (RB; 1951–54)
Montee Ball (RB; 2009–)
Marty Below (OT; 1922–23)
Tom Burke (DE; 1995–98)
Bob Butler (OT; 1911–13)
Ron Dayne (RB; 1996–99)
Lee Evans (WR; 1999–2001, 2003)
Jamar Fletcher (CB; 1998–2000)

Elroy "Crazy Legs" Hirsch (RB; 1942)
Pat O'Dea (P-PK-FB; 1896–99)
Cory Raymer (C; 1991–94)
Pat Richter (RB; 1960–62)
Dave Schreiner (WR; 1940–42)
Joe Thomas (OT; 2003–06)

KEY COACHES
Barry Alvarez (1990–2005):
    118–73–4; 8–3 (bowl games)
Phil King (1896–1902, 1905):
    65–11–1

HOME STADIUM
Camp Randall Stadium (1917–)

* All statistics through 2011 season

A man named Terry Westegard from the Wisconsin town of Portage got a bit too excited before a Badgers football game in 1976. Wearing a fur skirt and helmet, he joined the pompom team as it led cheers around Camp Randall Stadium. The response of the crowd was so positive, though, that Westegard continued doing the same routine at every home game through 1981. He became known as the Portage Plumber, though he was actually a steam fitter.

"What it means to be a Badger is more than athletic accomplishments. It's more than individual or team accomplishments. To me, it's who I am. It's who my family is. It's about the type of person that the university and the football program send out into the world." —Wisconsin offensive tackle Joe Thomas, who went on to star with the NFL's Cleveland Browns

Wisconsin "Kangaroo Kicker" Pat O'Dea boasted a stronger leg than other kickers of his era. He set a national record on November 25, 1898, by kicking a 62-yard field goal against Northwestern. According to records from that game, he also booted an 87-yard punt. The Badgers clobbered the Wildcats 27–0.

GLOSSARY

All-American
A player chosen as one of the best amateurs in the country in a particular activity.

athletic director
An administrator who oversees the coaches, players, and teams of an institution.

conference
In sports, a group of teams that plays each other each season.

draft
A system used by professional sports leagues to select new players in order to spread incoming talent among all teams. The NFL Draft is held each spring.

rankings
A system where voters rank the best teams in the country.

recruiting
Trying to entice a player to come to a certain school.

rival
An opponent that brings out great emotion in a team, its fans, and its players.

scholarship
Financial assistance awarded to students to help them pay for school. Top athletes earn scholarships to represent a college through its sports teams.

upset
A result where the supposedly worse team defeats the supposedly better team.

FOR MORE INFORMATION

FURTHER READING

Diemer, Lauren. *Rose Bowl (Sporting Championships)*. New York: Weigl Publishers, 2009.

Kaufman, Gabriel. *Football In The Big Ten*. Portland, OR: ReadHowYouWant, 2012.

Lucas, Mike. *The 25 Greatest Moments in Camp Randall History*. Stevens Point, WI: KCI Sports Publishing, 2005.

WEB LINKS

To learn more about the Wisconsin Badgers, visit ABDO Publishing Company online at **www.abdopublishing.com**. Web sites about the Badgers are featured on our Book Links page. These links are routinely monitored and updated to provide the most current information available.

PLACES TO VISIT

Camp Randall Stadium
1440 Monroe St.
Madison, WI, 53711
608-262-1866
www.uwbadgers.com/facilities/camp-randall.html

This is where Wisconsin has played its home games since 1917. Many of the finest players and coaches in the history of college football have graced this field over its nearly 100 years in existence.

College Football Hall of Fame
111 South St. Joseph St.
South Bend, IN 46601
1-800-440-FAME (3263)
www.collegefootball.org

This hall of fame and museum highlights the greatest players and moments in the history of college football. Among the former Badgers enshrined here are Heisman Trophy winner Alan Ameche, Elroy "Crazy Legs" Hirsch, Pat O'Dea, Pat Richter, and Dave Schreiner.

INDEX

Alvarez, Barry (coach), 10, 27–28, 30, 32, 33, 35, 36
Ameche, Alan, 22, 23, 24

Ball, Montee, 38, 39, 41
Beckum, Travis, 35, 36
Bevell, Darrell, 28, 30
Bielema, Bret (coach), 33, 35, 36, 37, 40
Bruhn, Milt (coach), 23–24
Bryant, Wendell, 6, 8
Burke, Tom, 6, 9–10
Butler, Bob, 14

Camp Randall Stadium, 13, 14–16, 38
Carimi, Gabe, 37, 38
Casillas, Jonathan, 35
Chambers, Chris, 10
Clay, John, 38
Coatta, John (coach), 24

Dayne, Ron, 6–8, 10, 32

Ellison, Kevin, 30
Evans, Lee, 32

Favret, John, 6
Fletcher, Jamar, 8, 32

Gilreath, David, 38

Harder, Pat, 17, 18
Hayden, Nick, 35
Henry, Aaron, 39
Hirsch, Elroy "Crazy Legs," 17, 18

James, Erasmus, 32
Jardine, John (coach), 24
Juneau, Bill (coach), 14

Levy, DeAndre, 35

McClain, Dave (coach), 24, 25, 28
Moffit, John, 38
Monty, Pete, 29
Moss, Brent, 29, 30

Nagy, Bill, 38

King, Phil (coach), 13–14

O'Dea, Pat "The Kangaroo Kicker," 14
"On, Wisconsin," 32

Pedersen, Jacob, 40

Raymer, Cory, 29
Richter, Pat, 23

Rose Bowl, 5–6, 8–9, 10–11, 22, 23, 29, 30, 31–32, 33, 39–41

Saleh, Tarek, 29
Samuel, Mike, 10, 11
Schreiner, Dave, 17, 22
Shaughnessy, Matt, 35
Spears, Clarence (coach), 16
Stocco, John, 36
Stuhldreher, Harry (coach), 18

Thistlethwaite, Glenn (coach), 16
Thomas, Joe, 35, 36, 37
Tillman, Dennis, 30
Tolzien, Scott, 40
Toon, Al, 40
Toon, Nick, 40

Watt, J. J., 38
White, James, 38
Wilson, Russell, 40–41
Wright, Randy, 25

ABOUT THE AUTHOR

Marty Gitlin is a freelance writer based in Cleveland, Ohio. He has written more than 60 educational books. Gitlin has won more than 45 awards during his 30 years as a writer, including first place for general excellence from the Associated Press. He lives with his wife and three children.